THE PA S
OF J

FOR CHILDREN

Written by Julianne Booth
Illustrated by Art Kirchhoff

ARCH® Books

MANUFACTURED IN THE UNITED STATES OF AMERICA

ISBN 0-570-06163-6

When Jesus on this earth did dwell,
Many a story He loved to tell.
We call them parables, and in each
Is a lesson Jesus wanted to teach.
When you hear these stories, keep in mind,
There's always a message for you to find.

When Jesus spoke of the kingdom of heaven,
He said, it's like a piece of leaven.
A little yeast will make bread rise,
Though it's small and hidden from your eyes.
The Kingdom is like a mustard seed;
Though tiny, it grows to be great indeed.
Some seeds grow in secret, there in the field,
But when harvest time comes, fine fruits they yield.

And while we're thinking of how crops grow,
Jesus told of a sower who went out to sow.
He scattered the seeds on the land all around,
Among weeds and rocks and on fertile ground.
As seeds in the good soil grew strong and true,
So the Kingdom takes root in the hearts of a few.

Like a pearl of great price is the Kingdom so fair.
Its worth is tremendous, beyond compare.
Like a treasure that's buried deep in the ground,
What joy and excitement come when it's found!
So it is with God's kingdom; when it becomes known,
One will sell all he has, to make it his own.

Like a house on a rock, standing firm in the storm,
Unshaken by wind and safe from all harm,
So is God's kingdom a foundation strong,
To keep you through trouble and guard you from wrong.

And Jesus proclaimed, when the End Time is near,
Like a fig tree in springtime, its signs will be clear.
The Kingdom is coming, and on that great day
We'll see who is chosen and who's turned away.

Like bad and good fish in a net from the deep,
Like weeds and good grain, like goats and like sheep,
So the evil and righteous are found side by side,
But the angels the good from the bad will divide.

Yes, many are called but the chosen are few,
For some people won't listen to teaching that's true.
Some folks are foolish, and some do not care,
So Jesus told parables warning, Prepare!

Don't be like the rich man who feasted in style,
As poor Lazarus sat at his gate all the while.
Then poor, simple Lazarus to heaven did go,
While the rich man found nothing but trouble and woe.

Don't be like the five girls whose lamps had no light,
So they couldn't go to a feast in the night.

Don't be like the woman who sewed a patch
Of new cloth on old, so they didn't match.
The garment tore worse, where the new cloth was basted.
Like new wine in old wineskins, everything wasted!

Don't be like the people invited to dine
At a rich man's house. They found cause to decline.
Because they were foolish, they missed a great treat,
While the rich man found others to come and eat.

Jesus taught this lesson again, and said,
There once was a king's son, about to be wed.
He sent invitations, but some folks said no,
They were busy with other things; they couldn't go.
So he sent for the humble, the poor, and the lame,
And they had a wonderful time when they came!

Don't be like the fool who built barns for his wealth
But gave no thought to his spiritual health.

But be like the servants on watch night and day
For their master's return from a land far away.
He's gone to a wedding feast, soon he'll be back;
His servants are waiting, they'll never be slack.
Wise is the steward who looks for his master;
He'll get his reward and avoid all disaster.
So Jesus teaches us—always hold steady,
The Kingdom is coming, we need to be ready.

A very sad parable tells of a fool
Who had not learned to practice the Golden Rule.
His master cancelled a great debt he owed,
But no thanks at all for this favor he showed.
For he, too, had a debtor whose payments did fail;
He took him to court and threw him in jail!
No mercy had he, but he got his just due
When his master threw him in prison, too!

Thus Jesus reminds us again and again,
God is disappointed when people sin.
But He's always glad when we cease to roam,
Like the Prodigal Son who at last came home.
He had wandered far, but his lesson he learned,
And his father forgave him when he returned.
So the angels in heaven rejoice, we are told,
Whenever a sinner returns to the fold.

To find a lost coin, the whole house you'll sweep,
As a shepherd will search for a little lost sheep.
Jesus, our Shepherd, wants us to live;
Jesus, our Savior, will always forgive.

Once there were two men who were both deep in debt,
One owed much more than the other, and yet
Their creditor cancelled both debts one fine day
And told them the money they need not repay.

Which one was more grateful? I'm sure that you know,
For the more that's forgiven, the more love we owe.

Jesus told of a fig tree with roots in the ground,
But nary a fig on its branches was found.
The owner said, "Let's chop down this bad tree."
But the gardener replied, "No, we'll just let it be.
Maybe next season good fruit it will bear.
It deserves one more chance before we despair!"

Does God answer prayers? people wanted to know.
And Jesus convinced them, it's certainly so.
If a friend at midnight came looking for you,
Knocking loudly—you'd hear him, and answer him too.
And like a judge hearing a poor widow's plea,
So God answers our prayers, as sure as can be.

But sometimes God's wisdom cannot be explained,
Like the great vineyard owner whose workers complainec
For all of these workers received the same pay,
Though some worked a few hours and others all day.
"Don' t complain," said the owner, "for one thing is true
It's not yours to question what I chose to do."

Then Jesus told of two men who did pray.
One said, "Lord, I'm just perfect in most every way!"
But the other man stood as meek as can be
And prayed, "Lord, have mercy on a sinner like me!"
Now, which one did better? I'm sure you can guess.
'Twas the poor humble sinner whom God did bless.

Like unworthy servants, we deserve no reward.
Nonetheless, true humility pleases the Lord.

A master gave money to his servants one day
And told them, "Invest it while I am away."
Whether talents or pounds, it was a great sum
For the servants to use till the master should come.
The wise ones obeyed him, but one man did not.
He said, "I might lose it; I'll hide what I've got."
He made a wrong choice. Jesus gives us the clues:
The gifts that God gave us, He wants us to use.
The man who had hidden his treasure away
Lost all that he had on the reckoning day.

So be like the steward who used what he had;
Because he was wise, his master was glad.

A man had two sons who both hated to work,
And often their duties these two men would shirk.
One morning the elder did loudly declare,
"I won't go to work today; I just don't care!"
But when he thought it over, he changed his plan
And went on to work like a good, honest man.
The younger son said, "I will work hard all day,"
But he took the day off and went on his way.
Which one did better? The elder, you see,
For actions speak louder than words, we agree.

A man fell among thieves as he traveled along.
They robbed him and beat him—a terrible wrong!
Some travelers saw him but quickly passed by.
If he didn't find help very soon, he would die!
Then there came to the rescue a wayfarer good,
A kindly Samaritan who helped all he could.
Jesus speaks with great praise of this man's noble deed
And the kindness he showed to another in need.

Now many of Jesus' stories we know,
And we think how He told them so long ago.
Better than treasures of silver and gold
Are these wonderful parables Jesus told.

DEAR PARENTS:

Our Savior, the Master Storyteller, repeatedly used parables to teach spiritual truths. You, as parents, have the privilege of introducing your children to these precious stories. They speak of God's kingdom, of His forgiving love, of how He answers prayer, of the Christian life, and of the coming judgment. In contrast to the self-righteousness of the Pharisees, Jesus emphasized mankind's sinfulness and God's grace—a most important lesson for all of us.

In the text we refer to the parables listed below. In the list we give the chapter and verse where each parable begins. You might find it interesting and profitable to look some of them up in your Bible.

As you go through this Arch Book with your child, stress God's forgiving and caring love for us, and the love we in turn should show to our fellowmen.

THE EDITOR

LIST OF PARABLES

1. Leaven, Matt. 13:33
   Mustard Seed, Matt. 13:31
   Seed Growing in Secret, Mark 4:26
2. Sower, Matt. 13:1
3. Goodly Pearl, Matt. 13:45
   Hidden Treasure, Matt. 13:44
4. House on Rock, Matt. 7:24
5. Fig Tree, Matt. 24:32
6. Draw Net, Matt. 13:47
   Tares, Matt. 13:24
   Sheep and Goats, Matt. 25:31
7. Rich Man and Lazarus, Luke 16:19
8. Ten Virgins, Matt. 25:1
9. New Cloth, Matt. 9:16
   New Wine in Old Bottles
   Matt. 9:17
10. Great Supper, Luke 14:16
11. Marriage of King's Son
    Matt. 22:2
12. Rich Fool, Luke 12:16
13. Watchful Servants, Luke 12:35
    Wise Steward, Luke 12:42
14. Unmerciful Servant, Matt. 18:23
15. Prodigal Son, Luke 15:11
16. Lost Coin, Luke 15:8
    Lost Sheep, Luke 15:3
17. Two Debtors, Luke 7:41
18. Barren Fig Tree, Luke 13:6
19. Friend at Midnight, Luke 11:5
    Unjust Judge, Luke 18:1
20. Laborers in Vineyard, Matt. 20:1
21. Pharisee and Publican, Luke 18:9
22. Unprofitable Servant, Luke 17:7
23. Talents, Matt. 25:14
    Pounds, Luke 19:12
24. Unjust Steward, Luke 16:1
25. Two Sons, Matt. 21:28
26. Good Samaritan, Luke 10:30